CRY OUT

Poets Protest the War

CRY OUT

Poets Protest the War

JULIA ALVAREZ · DAVID BUDBILL

GREG DELANTY · JODY GLADDING

DONALD HALL · JAMAICA KINCAID

GALWAY KINNELL · WILLIAM O'DALY

GRACE PALEY · JAY PARINI

RUTH STONE

George Braziller, Publisher · New York

in collaboration with Northshire Bookstore

Manchester, Vermont

First published by George Braziller, Inc., in 2003.

The copyright to each poem is held by its author, and permission to reprint
was granted by the author, unless noted otherwise on pp. 138-139.

For information, please address the publisher:

George Braziller, Inc.
171 Madison Avenue
New York, New York 10016

Printed and bound in the United States.

TO ALL THE YOUNG PEOPLE
SENT FORTH AS GLADIATORS,
AND TO ALL THE MEN, WOMEN, AND
CHILDREN WHO ARE TRIVIALIZED
AS THE "COLLATERAL DAMAGE"
OF WAR.

CONTENTS

9

STILL MARCHING

While attending a reading at the Northshire Bookstore honoring the right to protest, I listened to a poet read from a poem by Pablo Neruda about the Spanish Civil War; it was beautiful and strong:

> *from every socket of Spain*
> *Spain emerges*
> *And from every dead child a rifle with the eyes,*
> *And from every crime bullets are born*
> *Which will one day find the bull's eye of your hearts.*

I was eighteen years old when the Spanish Civil War broke out. Bombs fell on the people of Madrid and Barcelona, and we rallied in New York to defend the Spanish Republic. It was my first march for peace.

Then came World War II and more protests. Now I was in uniform, marching in an army this time, fortunate to come home in 1946. Within a few more years came Korea and another reason to march. But why did we march? For intervention? For pacifism? I imagine we were marching, filled with hope, for an end to all wars.

When we realized that more than fifty thousand young soldiers, and countless civilians, had died in Vietnam, we could tolerate the deaths no longer. This time, young men and women, who saw their own generation vanishing, cried out for an end.

It's 2003 and once again the threat of war hangs over us, despite all our efforts to resolve disputes by talking rather than killing. The protests seem larger now, more widespread, filled with people of all ages, races and nationalities. I look at news reports and realize that the streets of Jakarta suddenly resemble those of Melbourne, of Paris, of New York. The thousands of miles between San Francisco and Berlin have vanished. Injustice is recognized internationally.

Reflecting on history brings despair; so many young men and women – soldiers and civilians worldwide – have been lost. And yet, what if we had not protested against Vietnam? Would the death toll have reached one hundred thousand or more?

Now, though, we are protesting *before* the attack. History spurs our conscience. We march in numbers, from small church groups, city councils, and book clubs to cities, large and small. We are present as one body, and together with poets who have honored the right to protest throughout time and around the world, we cry out with one voice: Enough.

GEORGE BRAZILLER
February 2003

INTRODUCTION & THANKS

12   On February 16, 2003, Northshire Bookstore sponsored "A Poetry Reading to Honor the Right of Protest as a Patriotic and Historical American Tradition." This event was organized in response to the cancellation of the White House Poetry Symposium, and 750 people attended an evening of poetry and protest hosted by the First Congregational Church of Manchester, Vermont. The publisher, George Braziller, was one of those in the audience, and this book is the resulting collaboration between Northshire Bookstore and George Braziller, Inc.

Cry Out: Poets Protest the War presents the Northshire Bookstore event in written form. All proceeds from the sale of this book will benefit the American Booksellers Foundation for Freedom of Expression (ABFFE).

This event was made possible through the special efforts of Ed and Barbara Morrow, Chris Morrow, Zachary Marcus, Jessica Wood, Stan Hynds, Steven E. Berry, Gerrit Kouwenhoven, Bob Allen, the Northshire Bookstore staff, and many other volunteers from Manchester, Vermont.

Additional thanks to C-Span, "60 Minutes II," Green Mountain Video, Northshire Access Television, Vermont Public Radio, WAMC Radio, Capital District Progressive Radio, *The Los Angeles Times, Publisher's Weekly*, and numerous Vermont newspapers and magazines for all they did to make the event available to the community at large.

INTRODUCTORY REMARKS

STEVE BERRY: *Good afternoon, my name is Steve Berry and I am the minister here at the First Congregational Church of Manchester. Originally they were not called congregational churches; they were called "meeting houses." And the reason for that was very simple – it was the place where people used to meet. And that is what we are doing today. It's an old tradition that comes with a lot of ideas: worship, education, involvement, political activity, discussion, hearing and listening and learning . . . all part of the "meeting house tradition." So today we return to an earlier time, and, once again, think of what the "meeting house" meant in New England, and how that spread into the town meeting, and so on.*

The words of John Winthrop, first governor of the Bay Colony, are appropriate for us today. He cautions:

> *"If we do not restrain our individual appetites and ambitions, and put the good of the whole before the good of the self, if we are unable to share abundance with those in need, if we are unwilling to take our public responsibility more seriously than our private convenience, then this new society we are seeking to create will be no better than the one from which we are trying to escape. We will be an embarrassment to ourselves and to the world. We will be laughed at as fools on a foolish errand and we will deserve the ridicule and derision. If we cannot flourish together we will never flourish privately."*

In the society that Winthrop envisioned, the rich and poor, the high and the low, the leader and the led are knit together in a community of care and love. The law of love, which makes law bearable, supercedes all rules of governance.

"We must delight in each other, make other's conditions our own, rejoice together, mourn together, labor and suffer together – always having before our eyes our commission and community in the work as members of the same body. So shall we keep the unity of the spirit in the bond of peace."

So today we join in this "meeting house" to hear wonderful voices, and to punctuate the theme of our interdependence. Thanks to the co-owners of Northshire Bookstore, Ed and Barbara Morrow, marketing director Zachary Marcus, and all the other staff members of Northshire, this is being made possible. Please welcome Ed Morrow.

ED MORROW: *I'm Ed Morrow, co-owner, with my wife and sons, of the Northshire Bookstore. On behalf of the entire crew of the Northshire Bookstore, welcome to this special gathering. Thank you, Reverend Steve Berry, for providing this "meeting house" so that we may join in the global meeting that has been spontaneously convened this weekend to speak out on the issues of war and peace. The reasons we have assembled in this place are as numerous as there are people in the room. These reasons have been accumulating over the past many months, largely ignored, cast aside into a vat of seeming irrelevance – a vat now bubbling with a brew that will no longer be contained.*

The main reason that moved us at the Northshire to invoke this meeting is the love of the WORD. Words are mysterious marvels, and the ability to connect them meaningfully is a precious skill not to be muzzled. Beyond the craft of writing and communicating skillfully is the miraculous art of stitching words into a web that touches the very core of one's being. It is this art that we are celebrating and honoring today. And we are doing more. We seek to prevent the co-option of two words that have periodically in our history been sought for the exclusive use of zealots:

PATRIOTISM and LOYALTY.

In the face of new threats, both real and imagined, our history reveals a tendency for us to forget the principles upon which this country was founded. There are those who are willing to give up some of our cherished rights and freedoms. The very attributes that make our country great – that generate a respect and admiration around the globe. Even today, in "the Arab street," as the policy wonks and intelligence services refer to it, even today the rights and freedoms enjoyed by

Americans, are acknowledged, praised, and envied, in the Arab street.

Fifty years ago, the House Un-American Activities Committee – aptly named, for that is what it was engaged in – sought to usurp the right to define patriotism and loyalty. Protest and dissent played an essential role in the founding of our country, and they have been needed to keep our society free and open and governed by the rule of law. Our leaders are accountable to the people; that is a basic tenet in our form of government. Protest and dissent are tools of the people to hold our leaders accountable when we feel they've gone astray.

The generalized fear and sense of vulnerability generated by 9/11 has fostered a great expansion of governmental powers. Power is as corrupting here at home as it is anywhere else in the world. In a democracy, the citizenry is responsible for keeping this power in check, and that involves vocal dissent. Speaking out. Insisting on being heard. Protesting, if necessary. We are not being loyal to our country or our form of government if we refuse to protest or dissent when we believe policies are seriously askew. That may be loyalty to the people in office, but not to the country. So we refuse any corrupting dilution of the words "patriotism and loyalty" by honoring today, in this room, not merely the right, but the duty, to protest – to dissent. This we will do peacefully. This we will do together in a most uplifted manner, by sharing in a primary art.

Our erstwhile neighbor from down the road a bit, Robert Frost, called poetry "a way of remembering what it would imperil us to forget."

The spanking new Chairman of the National Endowment for the Arts, the poet Dana Gioia, suggests that the poet, who throughout the millennia has always stood at the very center of society, casts a gentle and benign spell, which allows us to access a deeper part of our humanity.

And now our director of spell casting, Zachary Marcus, will start the magic.

ZACHARY MARCUS: *In organizing this event, Galway Kinnell and I came up with the idea of a bit of 'democratic vaudeville,' meaning I will pick the names of the poets out of a hat at random. We will dispense with most bios and keep introductions to a minimum and allow the seamless flow of poetry to speak for itself.*

16

288

I'm Nobody! Who are you?
Are you – Nobody – Too?
Then there's a pair of us!
Don't tell! they'd advertise – you know!

How dreary – to be – Somebody!
How public – like a Frog –
To tell one's name – the livelong June –
To an admiring Bog!

EMILY DICKINSON

18   *During the Vietnam War, when I was teaching in Madison, Wisconsin,*
there were many student protests against that war. And rightly so. This
is a poem about a student of mine who was part of the protest and
ended up in jail.

LESSON

In the days when his mind was simple,
Before he learned the rules,
Sam A. was a pupil
In the orchards of the people.
He went to school.
Dense rhetoric and physics
And beards to hide the fools;
Napalm and pears and peaches
And marvelous cutting tools;
Ways and means, the National Guard,
And saffron submarines.

He leaned beyond his body
On an uncharted course.
Hairy and sick and sweating,
He earned the mind's inverse.
And bitter in his hide
With speed and speed and worse;
With oily glands and scales;
He lay on the floors and cried
In Madison's crowded jails.

In the days when his mind was simple,
Before he learned the rules,
Sam A. was a poet
In the orchards of the people.
And his agony was to know it,

Among the clean-shaven fools.
Naplam and pears and peaches,
We learn what the pupil teaches:
That the mind is the body's curse.
With his simian arm that reaches
Out to the universe.

20

RUTH STONE

EDEN, THEN AND NOW

In '29 before the dust storms
sandblasted
Indianapolis,
we believed in the milk company.
Milk came in glass bottles.
We spread dye colored butter,
now connected to cancer.
We worked seven to seven
with no overtime pay;
pledged allegiance every day,
pitied the starving Armenians.
One morning in the midst of plenty,
there were folks out of context,
who lived on nothing.
Some slept in shacks
on the banks of the river.
This phenomenon investors said
would pass away.
My father worked for the daily paper.
He was a union printer;
lead slugs and blue smoke.
He worked with hot lead
at a two ton machine,
in a low-slung seat;
a green billed cap
pulled low on his forehead.
He gave my mother a dollar a day.

You could say we were rich.
This was the jazz age.
All over the country
the dispossessed wandered
with their hungry children,
harassed by the law.

When the market broke, bad losers
jumped out the windows.
It was time to lay an elegant table,
as it is now; corporate paradise;
the apple before the rot caved in.
It was the same worm
eating the same fruit.
In fact, the same Eden.

RUTH STONE

MANTRA

When I am sad
I sing, remembering
the redwing blackbird's clack.
Then I want no thing
except to turn time back
to what I had
before love made me sad.

When I forget to weep,
I hear the peeping tree toads
creeping up the bark.
Love lies asleep
and dreams that everything
is in its golden net;
and I am caught there, too,
when I forget.

RUTH STONE

24   *I am proud to take part in this passionate occasion, sharing the passion with you, and a passion for peace, against our proposed terrible mis-adventure.*

I want to read a poem by Jane Kenyon, who would be here if she could – a poem that she wrote on an earlier Iraqi occasion.

THREE SMALL ORANGES

My old flannel nightgown, the elbows out,
one shoulder torn. . . . Instead of putting it
away with the clean wash, I cut it up
for rags, removing the arms and opening
their seams, scissoring across the breast
and upper back, then tearing the thin
cloth of the body into long rectangles.
Suddenly an immense sadness. . . .

Making supper, I listen to news
from the war, of torture where the air
is black at noon with burning oil,
and of a market in Baghdad, bombed
by accident, where yesterday an old man
carried in his basket a piece of fish
wrapped in paper and tied with string,
and three small hard green oranges.

JANE KENYON

26   *A poem by Walt Whitman called "Reconciliation." It is dated 1865-66 – a poem at the end of the war.*

RECONCILIATION

Word over all, beautiful as sky,
Beautiful that war and all its deeds of carnage must in time
    be utterly lost,
That the hands of the sisters Death and Night incessantly
    softly wash again, and ever again, this soil'd world;
For my enemy is dead, a man divine as myself is dead,
I look where he lies white-faced and still in the coffin – I
    draw near,
Bend down and touch lightly with my lips the white face in
    the coffin.

WALT WHITMAN

28 *Another tiny poem of Whitman's that I've always loved. It is dated 1865, and it is such a poem of peace.*

A FARM PICTURE

Through the ample door of the peaceful country barn,
A sunlit pasture field with cattle and horses feeding,
And haze and vista, and the far horizon fading away.

WALT WHITMAN

30   *I want to read a poem of my own that is about another war. It comes from memories of the Second World War, when I was a kid.*

1943

They toughened us for war. In the high school auditorium
Ed Moynahan knocked out Dominick Esposito in the first round

of the heavyweight finals, and ten months later Dom died
in the third wave at Tarawa. Every morning of the war

our Brock-Hall Dairy delivered milk from horse-drawn wagons
to wooden back porches in Southern Connecticut. In winter,

frozen cream lifted the cardboard lids of glass bottles,
Grade A or Grade B, while Marines bled to death in the surf,

or the right engine faltered into the Channel silt, or troops marched
– what could we do? – with frost-bitten feet as white as milk.

DONALD HALL

32   *I would like to thank Mrs. Bush for being so thin-skinned. If she had not been so thin-skinned we would not be sitting here. To think that a woman who goes to bed and sits down and has dinner with a man who is a lord and master of weapons of mass destruction, and plans to use them, could not stand to hear some poets disagree with him. When Walt Whitman and Emily Dickinson and Langston Hughes were chosen, you could see that they were chosen because they were dead, but we now bring them back to life. And we must never allow people like that to take them again. The next time you are asked by people in power to come and discuss great works of literature with them, you must tell them no. I am going to read a poem by Walt Whitman called "Proud Music of the Storm."*

PROUD MUSIC OF THE STORM

1

Proud music of the storm,
Blast that careers so free, whistling across the prairie,
Strong hum of forest tree-tops – wind of the mountains,
Personified dim shapes – you hidden orchestras,
You serenades of phantoms with instruments alert,
Blending with Nature's rhythmus all the tongues of nations;
You chords left as by vast composers – you choruses,
You formless, free, religious dances – you from the Orient,
You undertone of rivers, roar of pouring cataracts,
You sounds from distant guns with galloping cavalry,
Echoes of camps with all the different bugle-calls,
Trooping tumultuous, filling the midnight late, bending me
       powerless,
Entering my lonesome slumber-chamber, why have you
       seiz'd me?

2

Come forward O my soul, and let the rest retire,
Listen, lose not, it is toward thee they tend,
Parting the midnight, entering my slumber-chamber,
For thee they sing and dance O soul.

A festival song,
The duet of the bridegroom and the bride, a marriage-march,
With lips of love, and hearts of lovers fill'd to the brim with
       love,
The red-flush'd cheeks and perfumes, the cortege swarming
       full of friendly faces young and old,
To flutes' clear notes and sounding harps' cantabile.

Now loud approaching drums,
Victoria! see'st thou in powder-smoke the banners torn but
          flying? the rout of the baffled?
Hearest those shouts of a conquering army?

(Ah, soul, the sobs of women, the wounded groaning in
          agony,
The hiss and crackle of flames, the blacken'd ruins, the
          embers of cities,
The dirge and desolation of mankind.)

Now airs antique and mediaeval fill me,
I see and hear old harpers with their harps at Welsh festivals,
I hear the minnesingers singing their lays of love,
I hear the minstrels, gleemen, troubadours, of the middle ages.

Now the great organ sounds,
Tremulous, while underneath, (as the hid footholds of the
          earth,
on which arising rest, and leaping forward depend,
All shapes of beauty, grace, and strength, all hues we know,
Green blades of grass and warbling birds, children that
          gambol and play, the clouds of heaven above,)
The strong base stands, and its pulsations intermits not,
Bathing, supporting, merging all the rest, maternity of all
          the rest,
And with it every instrument in multitudes,
The players playing, all the world's musicians,
The solemn hymns and masses rousing adoration,
All passionate heart-chants, sorrowful appeals,
The measureless sweet vocalists of ages,
And for their solvent setting earth's own diapason,
Of winds and woods and mighty ocean waves,
A new composite orchestra, binder of years and climes, ten-
          fold renewer,
As of the far-back days the poets tell, the Paradiso,

The straying thence, the separation long, but now the
         wandering done,
The journey done, the journeyman come home,
And man and art with Nature fused again.

Tutti! for earth and heaven;
(The Almighty leader now for once has signal'd with his wand.)

The manly stophe of the husbands of the world,
And all the wives responding.

The tongues of violins,
(I think O tongues ye tell this heart, that cannot tell itself,
This brooding, yearning heart, that cannot tell itself.)

         3
Ah from a little child,
Thou knowest soul how to me all sounds became music,
My mother's voice in lullaby or hymn,
(The voice, O tender voices, memory's loving voices,
Last miracle of all, O dearest mother's, sister's, voices;)
The rain, the growing corn, the breeze along the long-
         leav'd corn,
The measur'd sea-surf beating on the sand,
The twittering bird, the hawk's sharp scream,
The wild-fowl's notes at night as flying low migrating north
         or south,
The psalm in the country church or mid the clustering trees,
         The open air camp-meeting,
The fiddler in the tavern, the glee, the long-strung sailor-song,
The lowing cattle, bleating sheep, the crowing cock at dawn.

All songs of current lands come sounding round me,
The German airs of friendship, wine and love,
Irish ballads, merry jigs and dances, English warbles,
Chansons of France, Scotch tunes, and o'er the rest,

Italia's peerless compositions.

Across the stage with pallor on her face, yet lurid passion,
Stalks Norma brandishing the dagger in her hand.

I see poor crazed Lucia's eyes' unnatural gleam,
Her hair down her back falls loose and dishevel'd.

I see where Ernani walking the bridal garden,
Amid the scent of night-roses, radiant, holding his bride by
        the hand,
Hears the infernal call, the death-pledge of the horn.

To crossing swords and gray hairs bared to heaven,
The clear electric base and baritone of the world,
The trombone duo, Libertad forever!

From Spanish chestnut trees' dense shade,
By old and heavy convent walls a wailing song,
Song of lost love, the torch of youth and life quench'd in
        despair,
Song of the dying swan, Fernando's heart is breaking.
Awaking from her woes at last retriev'd Amina sings,
Copious as stars and glad as morning light the torrents of
        her joy.

(The teeming lady comes,
The lustrious orb, Venus contralto, the blooming mother,
Sister of loftiest gods, Alboni's self I hear.)

4

I hear those odes, symphonies, operas,
I hear in the *William Tell* the music of an arous'd and angry
        people,
I hear Meyerbeer's *Huguenots,* the *Prophet*, or *Robert*,
Gounod's *Faust*, or Mozart's *Don Juan*.

I hear the dance-music of all nations,

The waltz, some delicious measure, lapsing, bathing me
          in bliss,
The bolero to tinkling guitars and clattering castanets.

I see religious dances old and new,
I hear the sound of the Hebrew lyre,
I see the crusaders marching bearing the cross on high to
          the martial clang of cymbals,
I hear the dervishes monotonously chanting, interspers'd with
          frantic shouts, as they spin around turning always
          towards Mecca,
I see rapt religious dances of the Persians and the Arabs,
Again, at Eleusis, home of Ceres, I see the modern Greeks
          dancing,
I hear them clapping their hands as they bend their bodies,
I hear the metrical shuffling of their feet.

I see again the wild old Corybantian dance, the performers
          wounding each other,
I see the Roman youth to the shrill sound of flageolets
          throwing and catching their weapons,
As they fall on their knees and rise again.

I hear from the Mussulman mosque the muezzin calling,
I see the worshippers within, nor form nor sermon,
          argument nor word,
But silent, strange, devout, rais'd, glowing heads, ecstatic faces.

I hear the Egyptian harp of many strings,
The primitive chants of the Nile boatman,
The sacred imperial hymns of China,
To the delicate sounds of the king, (the stricken wood and
          stone,)
Or to Hindu flutes and the fretting twang of the vina,
A band of bayaderes.

5

Now Asia, Africa leave me, Europe seizing inflates me,
To organs huge and bands I hear as from vast concourses of
        voices,
Luther's strong hymn, *Eine feste Burg ist unser Gott*,
Rossini's *Stabat Mater dolorosa*,
Or floating in some high cathedral dim with gorgeous
        color'd windows,
The passionate *Agnus Dei* or *Gloria in Excelsis*.

Composers! mighty maestros!
And you, sweet singers of old lands, soprani, tenori, bassi!
To you a new bard caroling in the West,
Obeisant sends his love.

(Such led to thee O soul,
All senses, shows and objects, lead to thee,
But now it seems to me sound leads o'er all the rest.)
I hear the annual singing of the children in St. Paul's
        cathedral,
Or, under the high roof of some colossal hall, the
        symphonies, oratorios of Beethoven, Handel, or Haydn,
The *Creation* in billows of godhood laves me.

Give me to hold all sounds, (I madly struggling cry,)
Fill me with all the voices of the universe,
Endow me with their throbbings, Nature's also,
The tempests, waters, winds, operas, and chants, marches and
        dances,
Utter, pour in, for I would take them all!

6

Then I woke softly,
And pausing, questioning awhile the music of my dream,
And questioning all those reminiscences, the tempest in its
        fury,

And all those songs of sopranos and tenors,
And those rapt oriental dances of religious fervor,
And the sweet varied instruments, and the diapason of
      organs,
And all the artless plaints of love and grief and death,
I said to my silent curious soul out of the bed of the
      slumber-chamber,
Come, for I have found the clew I sought so long,
Let us go forth refresh'd amid the day,
Cheerfully tallying life, walking around the world, the real,
Nourish'd henceforth by our celestial dream.

And I said, moreover,
Haply what thou hast heard O soul was not the sound of
      winds,
Nor dream of raging storm, nor sea-hawk's flapping wings
      nor harsh scream,
Nor vocalism of sun-bright Italy,
Nor German organ majestic, nor vast concourse of voices,
      nor layers of harmonies,
Nor strophes of husbands and wives, nor sound of marching
      soldiers,
Nor flutes, nor harps, nor the bugle-calls of camps,
But to a new rhythmus fitted for thee,
Poems bridging the way from Life to Death, vaguely wafted
      in night air, uncaught, unwritten,
Which lets us go forth in the bold day and write.

WALT WHITMAN

40

A WAKE ON LAKE CHAMPLAIN

As an F-16 unzips the sky
a white-sailed yacht races in
like a surrendering rider
from the plains of the lake & a boy
conjures doves with a piece of cake.

Gas pumps plug their fingers in their ears.
You can hardly hear a child start to cry.
Her father fails to rock her still.
Afterwards he remarks this jet is guarding
Plattsburgh Nuclear Base or on border drill.

Now she's mesmerized by a duck & drake
teaching paddling, oblivious fledgling
how to play follow-the-leader.
A peace sign spreads in their wake.

GREG DELANTY

HARLEM (A DREAM DEFERRED)

42   What happens to a dream deferred?

Does it dry up
like a raisin in the sun?
Or fester like a sore –
And then run?
Does it stink like rotten meat?
Or crust and sugar over –
like a syrupy sweet?

Maybe it just sags
like a heavy load.

Or does it explode?

LANGSTON HUGHES

INTERNATIONAL CALL

A hand holds a receiver out a top-storey window
in a darkening city. The phone is the black
old heavy type. From outside
what can we make of such an event?
The hand, which seems to be a woman's,
holds the phone away from her lover, refusing
to let him answer his high-powered business call.
More likely a mother has got one more
sky-high phone bill and in a tantrum warns
her phone-happy son she'll toss the contraption.
A demented widow, having cracked the number
to the afterlife, holds the receiver out
for the ghost of her lately deceased husband.
He's weary of heaven and wants to hear dusk birds,
particularly the excited choir of city starlings.
It's always dusk now, but the receiver isn't held out
to listen to the birds of the Earth from Heaven.
It's the black ear and mouth in the hand of a woman
as she asks her emigrated sisters and brothers
in a distant country if they can hear the strafing,
and those muffled thuds, how the last thud
made nothing of the hospital where they were slapped
into life. The hand withdraws. The window bangs closed.

The city is shut out. Inside now, the replaced phone
represses a moan. Its ear to the cradle
listens for something approaching from far off.

GREG DELANTY

44

THE ALIEN

I'm back again scrutinizing the Milky Way
       of your ultrasound, scanning the dark
            matter, the nothingness, that now the heads say
      is chockablock with quarks & squarks,
gravitons & gravitini, photons & photinos. Our sprout,

who art there inside the spacecraft
       of your ma, the time capsule of this printout,
            hurling & whirling towards us, it's all daft
      on this earth. Our alien who art in the heavens,
our Martian, our little green man, we're anxious

to make contact, to ask divers questions
       about the heavendom you hail from, to discuss
            the whole shebang of the beginning&end,
      the pre-big bang untime before you forget the why
and lie of thy first place. And, our friend,

to say Welcome, that we mean no harm, we'd die
       for you even, that we pray you're not here
            to subdue us, that we'd put away
      our ray guns, missiles, attitude and share
our world with you, little big head, if only you stay.

GREG DELANTY

46   *Before my last poem, I'd like to say that I would have welcomed a chance to go to the White House. I'd have to put on my collar and tie to show sameness rather than define myself as different, as I do when I attend demonstrations and when I do civil disobedience. We destructively define ourselves by difference all too often, and a demonstration with all the demonstrators dressed in suits rather than playing out the stereotypical conflict of the Denims versus the Suits would be very effective. I'd say, "Mr. Bush, all fire is friendly fire. You must stop looking at people as terrorists, because sooner rather than later, you'll turn into one yourself. Mr. President, now turn away from homo sapiens the terrorist and attend to the poor, the sick, the flora and the fauna of the world that we are undoing." But tonight I'm especially glad to be on this sublunar, crooked ball spinning through the multiverse of this universe – to be among this verse, this universe.*

THE SKUNK MOTHS

The family of skunks, their backs to me from our deck,
       are like great black & white caterpillars. I imagine them
the giant larvae of Luna moths or Monarch butterflies,
       their pupae unzipping and tremendous wings
unfolding, fluttering about the summer airways, big as people.
       And why not? I think we'd be frightened of such creatures,
each's revanchist proboscis, exacting retribution for the legions
       we've not let flutter down the summers? Imagine
their great eyes, big as cow eyes, gazing, gazing, gazing at us.
       Imagine the Luna's gossamer tulle wings, the tippets
brushing us, fanning us tenderly, wrapping us in a veil,
       bringing us gently to our knees in a gathering humility,
brushing aside our mortification, finally at home, natural
       in the natural world – their wings our cocoon – becoming
ourselves, pinioned resplendence, at last the human mothfly.

GREG DELANTY

48

TO THE STATES

To The States or any of them, or any city of The States,   49
      Resist much, obey little,
Once unquestioning obedience, once fully enslaved,
Once fully enslaved, no nation, state, city, of this earth, ever afterward
      resumes its liberty.

WALT WHITMAN

50   *I was talking to David Budbill about this next poem and he said,*
      "Hmmm, it seems the language of political debate in the 19th century
      was a little rougher than it is for us."

TO THE STATES

To Identify the 16th, 17th, or 18th Presidentiad

Why reclining, interrogating? Why myself and all drowsing?   51
What deepening twilight! Scum floating atop of the waters!
Who are they, as bats and night-dogs, askant in the Capitol?
What a filthy Presidentiad! (O south, your torrid suns! O north, your arctic
            freezings!)
Are those really Congressmen? Are those the great Judges? Is that the
            President?

Then I will sleep awhile yet – for I see that These States sleep, for reasons:
(With gathering murk – with muttering thunder and lambent shoots, we all
      duly awake,
South, north, east, west, inland and seaboard, we will surely awake).

WALT WHITMAN

52   *Emily Dickinson has this little perception and warning.*

#435

Much Madness is divinest Sense –   53
To a discerning Eye –
Much Sense – the starkest Madness –
'Tis the Majority
In this, as All, prevail –
Assent – and you are sane –
Demur – you're straightway dangerous –
And handled with a Chain –

EMILY DICKINSON

54   *I'm going read a few passages from this much longer poem of Walt Whitman's: "Poem of the Propositions of Nakedness." Most of Whitman's bitterness about America comes out in his prose, but occasionally it slips out in the poetry – and this is a kind of "Ginsbergian" rant. Whitman's bitterness, by the way, is not because he was a bitter person, or because he was anti-American or unpatriotic, but because he loved America so much that he was continually disappointed.*

Selections from

POEM OF THE PROPOSITIONS
OF NAKEDNESS

Let me bring this to a close – I pronounce openly for a new distribution of   55
     roles;
Let that which stood in front go behind! and let that which was behind
     advance to the front and speak. . .
Let men and women be mocked with bodies and mocked with Souls!
Let the love that waits in them, wait! let it die, or pass stillborn to other
     spheres!
Let the sympathy that waits in every man, wait! or let it also pass!. . .
Let the people sprawl with yearning, aimless hands! let their tongues be
     broken! let their eyes be discouraged! let none descend into their
     hearts with the fresh lusciousness of love!. . .
Let the theory of America still be management, caste, comparison! . . .
Let freedom prove no man's inalienable right! everyone who can tyrannize,
     let him tyrannize to his satisfaction! . . .
Let the eminence of meanness, treachery, sarcasm, hate, greed, be taken for
     granted above all! . . .
Let the white person again tread the black person under his heel!
Let the Asiatic, the African, the European, the American, and the Australian,
     go armed against the murderous stealthiness of each other! let them
     sleep armed! . . .
Let him who is without my poems be assassinated! . . .
Let all the men of These States stand aside for a few smouchers! let the few
     seize on what they choose! let the rest gawk, giggle, starve, obey! . . .
Let there be wealthy and immense cities – but still through any of them,
     not a single poet, savior, knower, lover!

WALT WHITMAN

56　　*This is a translation I made of Pablo Neruda. It's called "I Explain a Few Things." Neruda had been over to Spain during the Spanish Civil War when the Nazis were practicing for the Second World War, when they strafed the Spanish Republicans.*

I EXPLAIN A FEW THINGS

You will ask: But where are the lilacs?
and the metaphysics covered with poppies
and the rain that often struck
his words, filling them
with holes and birds?

Let me tell you what's happening with me.

I lived in a suburb,
of Madrid, with bells,
with clocks, with trees.

From there you could see
the parched face of Castile
like an ocean of leather.
                    My house was called
the house of flowers, because from everywhere
geraniums burst: it was
a beautiful house
with dogs and children.
                    Raul, do you remember?
Do you remember, Rafael?
                    Federico, under the ground,
do you remember my house with balconies
where the June light drowned the flowers in your mouth?
                              Brother, brother!

Everything
was loud voices, salt of goods,

crowds of pulsating bread,
in the market of my barrio of Arguelles, with its statue
like a pale inkwell set down among the hake:
a deep throbbing
of feet and hands filled the streets,
metres, liters, the harsh

measures of life,
                    Masses of fishes,
geometry of rooftops under a cold sun
in which the weather vane grows tired,
delirious fine ivory of potatoes,
tomatoes, more tomatoes, all the way to the sea.

And one morning it all was burning,
and one morning bonfires
sprang out of the earth
devouring humans,
and from then on fire,
gunpowder from then on,
and from then on blood.
Banditos with planes and Moors,
banditos with rings and duchesses,
banditos with black friars making the sign of the cross,
came down from the sky to kill children
and the blood of children ran through the streets
simply, like the blood of children.

Jackals the jackals would despise,
stones the dry thistle would bite on and spit out,
vipers the vipers would abominate!

Facing you, I have seen the blood
of Spain rise up like a tide
to drown you in a single wave
of pride and knives!

Traitors,
generals:
look at my dead house,
look at Spain broken:
from every house flaming metal bursts
instead of flowers,
from every crater of Spain

comes Spain,
from every dead child comes a rifle with eyes,
from every crime bullets are born
which will one day find in you
the site of the heart.

You will ask: Why doesn't his poetry
speak to us of dreams, of leaves,
of the great volcanoes of his native land?

Come and see the blood in the streets.
Come and see
the blood in the streets,
come and see the blood
in the streets!

PABLO NERUDA

60 *And, finally, a little poem of mine that bears on what is now called "col-lateral damage," of which we fear there would be much in an invasion of Iraq. This poem was not written for this occasion but during the Viet-nam War. Fergus, my son, was then one year old.*

THE OLIVE WOOD FIRE

Majorca, winter 1970

When Fergus woke crying at night,
I would carry him from his crib
to the rocking chair and sit holding him
before the fire of thousand-year-old olive wood.
Sometimes, for reasons I never knew
and he has forgotten, even after his bottle the big tears
would keep on rolling down his big cheeks
— the left cheek always more brilliant than the right —
and we would sit, some nights for hours, rocking
in the light eking itself out of the ancient wood,
and hold each other against the darkness,
his close behind and far away in the future,
mine I imagined all around.
One such time, fallen half asleep myself,
I thought I heard a scream
— a flier crying out in horror
as he dropped fire on he didn't know what or whom,
or else a child thus set aflame —
and sat up alert. The olive wood fire
had burned low. In my arms lay this child,
fast asleep, left cheek glowing, God.

GALWAY KINNELL

62

My first poem is a translation of Gabriela Mistral's "Land of Absence." Gabriela Mistral, Chilean Nobel laureate, fabulous teacher by all accounts, took the penname of Gabriela Mistral because she was worried that if people knew she was writing such emotionally outspoken verses, she would lose her job.

The second poem was written by a grade school student of Gabriela Mistral, Pablo Neruda. This is in my translation from Neruda's book, Winter Garden. *It is also a poem of disappointment. Neruda believed that the place of religion in our lives was to help us ask questions, not to answer all of them for us, but to learn to live with them.*

LAND OF ABSENCE

Land of absence,
strange land,
lighter than angel
or subtle sound,
color of dead algae,
color of falcon,
with the age of all time,
with no age content.

It bears no pomegranate
nor grows jasmine,
and has no skies
nor indigo seas.
Its name, a name
that has never been heard,
and in a land without name
I shall die.

Neither bridge nor boat
brought me here.
Nobody told me
it was island or shore.
A land I did not search for
and did not discover.

Like a fable
that I learned,
a dream of taking

and letting go,
and it is my land
where I live and I die.

It was born to me of things
that are not of land,
of kingdoms and kingdoms
that I had and I lost,
of all things living
that I have seen die,
of all that was mine
and went from me.

I lost ranges of mountains
wherein I could sleep.
I lost orchards of gold
that were sweet to live.
I lost islands of indigo
and sugar cane,
and the shadows of these
I saw circling me,
and together and loving
become a land.

I saw manes of fog
without back or nape,
saw sleeping breaths
pursue me,
and in years of wandering
become a land,
and in a land without name
I shall die.

GABRIELA MISTRAL

GAUTAMA CHRIST

66   The names of God and especially of his representative
called Jesus or Christ, according to texts and mouths,
have been used up, worn down and deposited
on the riverbank of our lives
like empty mollusk shells.
Nevertheless, touching these sacred names
drained of their blood, wounded petals,
balances of the oceans of love and of fear,
we know something endures there: an agate lip,
an iridescent footprint still shimmering in the light.

While the names of God were spoken
by the best and the worst, by the clean and the dirty,
by whites and blacks, by blood-stained assassins
and golden brown victims who blazed with napalm,
while Nixon with the hands
of Cain blessed those he had condemned to death,
when fewer and smaller divine footprints were found on the beach,
men began to examine the colors,
the promise of honey, the symbol for uranium,
with suspicion and hope they studied the possibilities
of killing and not killing each other, of organizing themselves in rows,
of going even further, of making themselves limitless, without rest.

We who live through these ages with their bloody flavor,
the smell of smoking rubble, of dead ash,
we who were not able to forget the sight
have often stopped to think in the names of God,
have raised them up tenderly, because they reminded us

of our ancestors, of the first humans, of those who asked questions,
of those who found the hymn that united them in misery
and now seeing the empty fragments where that man lived
we finger those smooth substances
spent, squandered by good and evil.

PABLO NERUDA

68   *This is a poem of my own that I wrote for the "Poets Against the War" website. There are a number of quotations in this poem, ranging from George W. Bush to my five-year-old daughter. I'll leave it to you to fig-ure out which are the most coherent.*

TO THE FORTY-THIRD PRESIDENT OF THE UNITED STATES OF AMERICA

Mr. President, our history speaks to us, the history of Chile
and China, El Salvador and Nicaragua, Somalia, Puerto Rico –
today, our solemn duty is to defy your willful aggression,
to parse provocative words and habits, your heroic battle
to distract us. Perhaps you think God will protect us
from the religious zealots who sanctify your rule,
from your opportunism and the race renewal,
the investiture you have assumed because, as
always, it is not yours. Let me ask
an obvious question.

                         If we are to establish peace
and security for our nation, must we not do
everything in our power to end
the beginnings of war, must we not allow
our imaginations to craft a lasting peace?
Are not the children you would choose
to incinerate our own? We try on masks
to trick our isolated, frightened selves,
to propagate our sacred uncertainties
among the children of this blue planet,
a world we create and ruin every day.
                                 Mr. President,
where do we walk, where may we sit down,
where can we work or rest, weep or pray,
what field does a man sunder and seed
in a country living only in memory, dying
every day at the hands of those who profess
to love her most? They say God loves America,

and that this "old bitch gone in the teeth" is
heaven on earth; in preemptive violence,
in obstinacy, in entitlements for the rich,
this murdered land, this, the people's
earth, is our reward for being right
no matter how wrong we are.

                              What "urge and rage"
thrives in the American heart, that so many cheer
this obsessive, unilateral madness?

                              Even through
precise layers of glass, the TV peddling
a thrilling efficiency, we cannot see them,
the ghosts that inhabit our malnourished
statistics, inhospitable closets, cold kitchens
where we eat meat and raise goblets of wine
to celebrate our belief that they are not like us.
I want to spend more time with my daughter,
my five-year-old, I want to see her, to know
she is alive. It is her "evening of the morning,"
she is just fine, though she implores me to tell her
the "acommitation of naked truth."

                              I imagine
Iraqis, weakened by sanctions, spending time
with their children. What do they play together,
what makes them laugh, what crude medicine
do parents spoon down fevered throats, when
they, too, are roused from nightmares of fragile
necklaces of bone, slung around the necks of
American fighters whose hearts we camouflage?
Who will witness the small charred bodies floating
in the Tigris, children writhing in pain, in smoking rubble,
in the ruins of Bab al-Wastani or the Mirjan Mosque,
severed limbs and glazed eyes that last night
followed their favorite story by candlelight?

                                          Mr. President,
what does it mean when you say Saddam Hussein,
Butcher of Baghdad, official liar, terrorizes himself?
It he brings terror upon himself, will our dark angels
exterminate him or his already wounded people;
and would you answer Mr. Korb: What if Kuwait grew carrots, what
if Iraq's main exports were chick peas and cotton shawls   71
destined for American women
longing for the exotic?
                        To be honest,
I have forgotten from what we must abstain,
yet we know how to prevent conception. *"C'est la vie,"*
you say, saddled up, ready to ride with your posse
across oil fields just like those in Texas.
It appears the one thing we cherish
more than petroleum or our children
is the greased machinery of destruction.

WILLIAM O'DALY

DAVID BUDBILL

72

A LITTLE STORY ABOUT AN ANCIENT CHINESE EMPEROR

Thousands of years ago in ancient China a boy emperor ruled for awhile.
The Imperial Court had placed the child on the throne so that he could be
a mouthpiece for the Imperial Court's desires.

Coddled from birth, surrounded by servants and sycophants,
told by the Imperial Court that he was The Son of Heaven,
given to believe he had no obligation to anyone but his Imperial Court,
pampered and protected from any notion of what the real world was like,
from any idea of what The People had to put up with every day,

The Emperor stomped and swaggered through the world
telling The People what to do, taking whatever he wanted,
robbing from the poor and giving to the rich, and sending
his armies out to terrorize whomever he took a notion to despise.

The Emperor ruled for a long time and thousands of The People
died, killed by his armies and because of his abuse and neglect.
But eventually, after great suffering, The People rose up and
crushed the man who called himself The Son of Heaven.
And they crushed his Imperial Court as well.

Then some time passed in which The People lived in relative calm
until another Emperor, like the one in this story, came along.

DAVID BUDBILL

EASY AS PIE

74   The Emperor divides the world
      into two parts:
      the Good and the Evil.

      If you don't accept that,
      The Emperor says
      you are Evil.

      The Emperor declares himself
      and his friends:
      Good.

      The Emperor says as soon as
      Good has destroyed Evil,
      all will be Good.

      Simple as one, two, three.
      Clear as night and day.
      Different as black and white.

      Easy as pie.

      DAVID BUDBILL

NO ESCAPE

I hung in there as long as I could, endured bedlam   75
on the ship of state as long as possible, and then
on a summer day in 1969 at the age of twenty-nine,
having known riots, assassinations, wars and mere
anarchy loosed upon the streets, I jumped overboard
and swam all the way up here to Judevine Mountain
to where, as Han Shan said, I thought I might
dwell and gaze in freedom.

It's more than thirty years later now and still I know
it is impossible to leave my country. Even though I live
among these cliffs hidden by the clouds, there is still
nowhere I can hide from the way The Emperor
and his bullies beat up on the world.

DAVID BUDBILL

from

WHEN LILACS LAST IN THE DOORYARD BLOOM'D

76   And I saw askant the armies,
And I saw as in noiseless dreams, hundreds of battle-flags,
Borne through the smoke of the battles and pierced with missiles I saw
        them,
And carried hither and yon through the smoke, and torn and bloody,
And at last but a few shreds left on the staffs, (and all in silence,)
And the staffs all splinter'd and broken.

I saw battle-corpses, myriads of them,
And the white skeletons of young men – I saw them,
I saw debris and debris of all the slain soldiers of the war,
But I saw they were not as was thought,
They themselves were fully at rest – they suffer'd not,
The living remain'd and suffer'd, the mother suffer'd,
And the wife and the child, and the musing comrade suffer'd,
And the armies that remain'd suffer'd.

WALT WHITMAN

HOW FEW OF US ARE LEFT, HOW FEW!

How few of us are left, how few!   77
Why do we not go back?
Were it not for our prince and his concerns,
What should we be doing here in the dew?

How few of us are left, how few!
Why do we not go back?
Were it not for our prince's own concerns,
What should we be doing here in the mud?

ANONYMOUS   Chinese, 1000 to 600 B.C.E.

MOTHER IN WARTIME

78

As if it were some noble thing,
She spoke of sons at war,
As if freedom's cause
Were pled anew at some heroic bar,
As if the weapons used today
Killed with great élan,
As if Technicolor banners flew
To honor modern man –
Believing everything she read
In the daily news,
(No in-between to choose)
She thought that only
One side won,
Not that *both*
Might lose.

LANGSTON HUGHES

PEACE

We passed their graves:
The dead men there,
Winners or losers,
Did not care.

In the dark
They could not see
Who had gained
The victory.

LANGSTON HUGHES

OFFICIAL NOTICE

80   Dear Death:
        I got your message
        That my son is dead.
        The ink you used
        To write it
        Is the blood he bled.
        You say he died with honor
        On the battlefield,
        And that I am honored, too,
        By this bloody yield.
        Your letter
        Signed in blood,
        With his blood
        Is sealed.

        LANGSTON HUGHES

WHAT ISSA HEARD

Two hundred years ago Issa heard the morning birds
singing sutras to this suffering world.

I heard them too, this morning, which must mean

since we will always have a suffering world
we must also always have a song.

God bless the people of Iraq

As-Salaam-Alaikum, Iraq

As-Salaam-Alaikum, Iraq

As-Salaam-Alaikum

DAVID BUDBILL

I want to start with a poem that is a message from Hopi Elders to their young people during a difficult time in their history, and I think it is appropriate for us now.

In the gloom and doom of late December, 2002, feeling heavy-hearted at the thought of what awaited us in the new year, this Message From the Hopi Elders, arrived in a holiday letter from my friend, the activist and writer Margaret Randall. Reading it I felt inspired by the words of a community that had suffered the horrors of war, genocide, and dis-placement. There was hope. But I had to be one of the people I was waiting for.

MESSAGE FROM
THE HOPI ELDERS

You must go back and tell the people that this is the Hour.
And there are things to be considered.

Where are you living?
What are you doing?
What are your relationships?
Are you in right relation?
Where is your water?
Know your garden.
It is time to speak your truth.
Create your community.
Be good to each other.
And do not look outside yourself for the leader.

This could be a good time! There is a river flowing now
very fast. It is so great and swift that there are those who
will be afraid. They will try to hold on to the shore. They
will feel they are being torn apart and will suffer greatly.

See who is there with you and celebrate. At this time in
history, we are to take nothing personally. Least of all,
ourselves. For the moment that we do, our spiritual
growth and journey comes to a halt.

The time of the lone wolf is over. Gather yourselves!
Banish the word struggle from your attitude and your
vocabulary. All that we do now must be done in a sacred
        manner and in celebration.

We are the ones we have been waiting for.

HOPI ELDERS

This little poem by Langston Hughes, "I, Too, Sing America," is an iconic poem for me. It is a poem in which Langston Hughes promises that he will be invited to the table of American literature. In view of the "disinvitation" to the table of the White House poets, it seems an appropriate poem to read tonight.

I, TOO

I, too, sing America

I am the darker brother.
They send me to eat in the kitchen
When company comes,
But I laugh
And eat well,
And grow strong.

Tomorrow,
I'll be at the table
When company comes.
Nobody'll dare
Say to me,
"Eat in the kitchen,"
Then.

Besides,
They'll see how beautiful I am
And be ashamed –

I, too, am America.

LANGSTON HUGHES

86   *This is a poem I wrote upon hearing that Sam Hamill and the other poets had been disinvited to the White House.*

THE WHITE HOUSE HAS DISINVITED THE POETS

The White House has disinvited the poets
to a cultural tea in honor of poetry
after the Secret Service got wind of a plot
to fill Mrs. Bush's ears with anti-war verse.
Were they afraid the poets might persuade
a sensitive girl who always loved to read,
a librarian who stocked the shelves with Poe
and Dickinson? Or was she herself afraid
to be swayed by the cooing doves and live at odds
with the screaming hawks in her family?

The Latina maids are putting away the cups
and the silver spoons, sad to be missing out
on *música* they seldom get to hear
in the hallowed halls. . . The valet sighs
as he rolls the carpets up and dusts the blinds.
Damn but a little Langston would be good
in this dreary mausoleum of a place!
Why does the White House have to be so white?
The chef from Baton Rouge is starved for verse
uncensored by Homeland Security.

No Poetry Until Further Notice!
Instead the rooms are vacuumed and set up
for closed-door meetings planning an attack
against the ones who always bear the brunt
of silencing: the poor, the powerless,
the ones who serve, those bearing poems, not arms.
So why be afraid of us, Mrs. Bush?
you're married to a scarier fellow.
We bring you the tidings of great joy –
not only peace but poetry on earth.

JULIA ALVAREZ

One last poem. Many of you may know the poem by Auden in which the line occurs: "Poetry makes nothing happen," which he doesn't mean. So the title of this one is that Auden quote, "Poetry Makes Nothing Happen," but I add a question mark: "Poetry Makes Nothing Happen"?

"POETRY MAKES NOTHING HAPPEN"?

W. H. Auden

Listening to a poem on the radio,
Mike Holmquist stayed awake on his drive home
from Laramie on Interstate 80,
tapping his hand to the beat of some lines
by Longfellow; while overcome by grief
one lonesome night when the bathroom cabinet
still held her husband's meds, May Quinn reached out
for a book by Yeats instead and fell asleep
cradling "When You Are Old," not the poet's best,
but still . . . poetry made nothing happen,

which was good, given what May had in mind.
Writing a paper on a Bishop poem,
Jenny Klein missed her ride but arrived home
to the cancer news in a better frame of mind.
While troops dropped down into Afghanistan
in the living room, Naomi Stella clapped
to the nursery rhyme her father had turned on,
All the king's horses and all the king's men . . .
If only poetry had made nothing happen!
If only the president had listened to Auden!

Faith Chaney, Lulú Pérez, Sunghee Chen—
there's a list as long as an epic poem
of folks who'll swear a poem has never done
a thing for them. . . except. . . perhaps adjust
the sunset view one cloudy afternoon,
which made them see themselves or see the world
in a different light – degrees of change so small
only a poem registers them at all.
That's why they can be trusted, why poems might
still save us from what happens in the world.

JULIA ALVAREZ   *for Jay Parini*

90   *People have been asking me for, oh, the last five years or so: "At your*
age, do you have any hope for things? I mean, what do you think about
things?" And so I really ransacked my mind for hope and came up with
very little. It seemed to me that the world was in about as worse a situa-
tion as it has been in my lifetime. With the proliferation of weapons of
destruction, which "what's his name" seems to think that Saddam has
them all, it's kind of interesting – I guess nobody in the secret service
told him where ours are. But the protests that have happened in the last
few days are so encouraging – so hope-making. I really feel that the rise
of the poets has had a lot to do with it. I really do. I want to read a
couple of peace poems of Walt Whitman.

from
SONG OF MYSELF

Twenty-eight young men bathe by the shore,
Twenty-eight young men and all so friendly;
Twenty-eight years of womanly life and all so lonesome.
She owns the fine house by the rise of the bank,
She hides handsome and richly drest aft the blinds of the window.

Which of the young men does she like the best?
Ah the homeliest of them is beautiful to her.

Where are you off to, lady? For I see you,
You splash in the water there, yet stay stock still in your room.

Dancing and laughing along the beach came the twenty-ninth bather,
The rest did not see her, but she saw them and loved them.

The beards of the young men glisten'd with wet, it ran from their long hair,
Little streams pass'd all over their bodies.

An Unseen hand also pass'd over their bodies,
It descended trembling from their temples and ribs.

The young men float on their backs, their white bellies bulge to the sun,
They do not ask who seizes fast to them,

They do not know who puffs and declines with pendant and bending arch,
They do not think whom they souse with spray.

WALT WHITMAN

I HEAR IT WAS CHARGED
AGAINST ME

92   I hear it was charged against me that I sought to destroy
institutions,
but really I am neither for or against institutions,
(What indeed have I in common with them? or what with the destruction
      of them?)
Only I will establish in the Mannahatta and in every city of
these states inland and seaboard,
And in the fields and woods, and above every keep little or
large that dents the water,
Without edifices or rules or trustees or any argument,
The institution of the dear love of comrades.

WALT WHITMAN

GOOD MORNING

Good morning, daddy!
I was born here, he said,
watched Harlem grow
until colored folks spread
from river to river
across the middle of Manhattan
out of Penn Station
dark tenth of a nation,
planes from Puerto Rico,
and holds of boats, chico,
up from Cuba Haiti Jamaica,
in buses marked New York
from Georgia Florida Louisiana
to Harlem Brooklyn the Bronx
but most of all to Harlem
dusky sash across Manhattan
    I've seen them come dark
    wondering
    wide-eyed
dreaming
out of Penn Station –
but the trains are late.
The gates are open –
Yet there're bars
at each gate.
    What happens
to a dream deferred?

Daddy, ain't you heard?

LANGSTON HUGHES

94   *I'm going to read a couple of my poems. The first one is an older poem that I wrote about Vietnam in 1971. I'd been there in '69 and really seen what the invention of the airplane could do to the world, the total destruction. I came back and sat on my hill here in Vermont and wrote this poem.*

CONNECTIONS:
VERMONT VIETNAM

The generals came to the president
We are the laughing stock of the world
What world? he said
                          the world
                          the world

Vermont
the green world
the green mountain

Across the valley
someone is clearing a field
he is making a tan rectangle
he has cut a tan rectangle on Lyme Hill
the dark wood
the deposed farm
                          the mist is sipped up by the sun
                          the mist is eaten by the sun
What world? he said

What mountain? said the twenty ships of the Seventh Fleet
rolling on the warm waves lobbing shells all the summer day
into green distance

                  On Trung Son mountain Phan Su told a joke
                  The mountain is torn, the trees are broken
                  How easy it is to gather wood
                  To repair my house in the village which is broken by bombs

His shirt is plum-colored is brown like dark plums
the sails on the sampans that fish in the sea of the Seventh Fleet
are plum colored
the holes in the mountain are red
the earth of that province is red red
world

GRACE PALEY

FATHERS

Fathers are
more fathering
these days they have
accomplished this by
being more mothering

what luck for them that
women's lib happened then
the drama of new fathering
began to shine in the eyes
of free women and was
irresistible

on the New York subways
and the mass transits
of other cities one may
see fatherings of many colors
with their round babies on
their laps this may also
happen in the countryside

these scenes were brand new
exciting for an old woman who
had watched the old fathers
gathering once again in
familiar army camps and com-
fortable war rooms to consider
the eradication of
the new fathering fathers
(who are their sons) as well
as the women and children who
will surely be in the way

GRACE PALEY

98

#560

It knew no lapse, nor Dimunition –
But large – serene –
Burned on – until through Dissolution –
It failed from Men –

I could not deem these Planetary forces
Annulled –
But suffered an Exchange of Territory
Or World –

EMILY DICKINSON

I want to read a few parts of a poem by George Oppen, another great American poet who won't be celebrated in this White House. George Oppen served as an infantryman in World War II, and when he returned to the States he was forced into exile in Mexico because of McCarthy. This is from his long poem "Of Being Numerous," which was published in a volume of the same name during the Vietnam War in 1968, a book that won the Pulitzer prize the following year. Another interesting thing about Oppen was that he stopped writing for about 25 years and organized. He was a communist and decided that writing was not the important work to be done in that time, and only wrote again when he felt like he could. He is a good model for how we need to balance the power of words and the power of action.

Excerpts from

OF BEING NUMEROUS

14

I cannot even now
Altogether disengage myself
From those men

With whom I stood in emplacements, in mess tents,
In hospitals and sheds and hid in the gullies
Of blasted roads in a ruined country,

Among them many men
More capable than I –

Muykut and a sergeant
Named Healy,
That lieutenant also –

How forget that? How talk
Distantly of 'The People'

Who are that force
Within the walls
Of cities

Wherein their cars

Echo like history
Down walled avenues
In which one cannot speak.

18

It is the air of atrocity,
An event as ordinary
As a President.

A plume of smoke, visible at a distance
In which people burn.

– They await

War, and the news
Is war

As always

That the juices may flow in them
Tho the juices lie.

Great things have happened
On the earth and given it history, armies
And the ragged hordes moving and the passions
Of that death. But who escapes
Death

Among these riders
Of the subway,

They know
By now as I know

Failure and the guilt
Of failure
As in Hardy's poem of Christmas

We might half-hope to find the animals
In the sheds of a nation
Kneeling at midnight,

Farm animals,
Draft animals, beasts for slaughter
Because it would mean they have forgiven us,
Or which is the same thing,
That we do not altogether matter.

40

Whitman: 'April 19, 1864

The capitol grows upon one in time, especially as they have got the
great figure on top of it now, and you can see it very well. It is a great
bronze figure, the Genius of Liberty I suppose. It looks wonderful toward sundown. I love to go and look at it. The sun when it is nearly
down shines on the headpiece and it dazzles and glistens like a big star:
it looks quite

103

curious . . .'

GEORGE OPPEN

104   *I'm going to end with a couple poems of my own. The first is called*
        "Jack and the Beanstalk." It's a study of the complicity of the wives of
        powerful men.

JACK AND THE BEAN STALK

"Not being altogether bad, she let him in and gave him breakfast."

My husband does eat men, she tells Jack
before she hides him in the oven
where the last scrawny beggar

was baked. It's still warm. The giant
smells Jack's sweat, but the giant's wife lies
and bustles him through

the kitchen. How did it come
to this – deceiving an ogre to safeguard
a thief? What was it she wanted?

To accommodate, only that. Or
to escape unnoticed, more
difficult for so large

 a woman. Now finding
herself intimate with
the unthinkable, all she can do

is make the best of things.
He gives her something to hide
behind, at least, his shadow

the lengthy excuse she never has
to finish. He calls her little
woman and keeps her in skins

and his atrocities fill up the space
around her well-dressed frame
neat as a page

from the Sunday Times. Oh, he loves
to fo and fum and hand down
a string of limp bodies.

When it comes to Englishmen,
though, there she draws the line.
He has to make his own grisly bread.

But she butters it. She finishes the crusts.

JODY GLADDING

FORE FATHERS

Are they helping with the library sale?
Are they waiting for the busses?
Did they send along the sunscreen?
Have they gone on the field trip?
Are they providing the refreshments?
Have they signed the permission forms?

They've taken the day off.
They've gathered to look under the hood.
They're trying to get their little white balls into all eighteen holes.

JODY GLADDING

108

It's important for all of us to be standing up talking. You're standing up by being here. We have a president who's about to kill, to burn, and dismember tens of thousands of Iraqi children, mothers, fathers, and innocent American soldiers who probably don't know what they're doing out there. And this is going to come back to us for generations to come. We're paying for this with American dollars, which they're borrowing from our children and our children's children. So I come here tonight, I'm sorry to say, more in anger than anything. We're here to say that we are very, very upset about what's going on in the world today, and we join today with the voices of the millions around the world who are marching with us against this crazy drive to war.

Poets are always the conscience of the people; poetry is the conscience of the people. Not individual poets, they don't matter. Poetry matters, the conscience of language which has been distilled and made pure by thought and care and love. Whitman was one of our greatest consciences. He wrote in Calamus,

> *The poet says indifferently and the like, 'How are you, friend?' He says this to the president and he says, 'Goodbye my brother' to the man who works in the sugar field. And both understand him and know that his speech is right. The maker of poems settles justice, reality, immortality. His insight and power encircle things in the human race. He is the glory and the extract thus far of things and of the human race.*

Poetry really does matter, and it matters most in these times of peril. As Auden said, "All I have is a voice to undo the folded lie." And that's what we're working for, we're working to undo that folded lie. Here is a poem I wrote called "In Time of War."

IN TIME OF WAR

We all moved easily within our borders;
you could almost not believe a war
was really going on, though fighters flew
in pairs across the lake and over mountains
and one saw the troops in restaurants
and sometimes in the streets, always polite.

The President assured us all was well.
He had made some eloquent addresses
in the months before the war began.
Now intermittently we heard that victory
was near at hand, that soon the enemy
would fold its tents, pull down its fences.

Children were all taught the patriotic songs.
They sang them in the streets. Employment
in the factories was full, though wages sank.
The Boy Scouts marched in serried ranks
in parks, while Girl Scouts baked their cookies
for young men far away and fighting.

You could still get many distant channels
on the pay TV. A few of them brought
pictures of the war: the refugees who
failed to cross the borders, accidental deaths
in hospitals and streets, the burning tires
and blazing trees and scattering of tribes.

We heard the tallies and assumed the best,
believing in the cycles that must spin,
that war is just a prelude to the peace
that always passes understanding. History
was happy with this pattern, which it knew
by heart, wiping the blood from its big chops.

JAY PARINI

AFTER THE TERROR

Everything has changed, though nothing has.
They've changed the locks on almost every door,
and windows have been bolted just in case:

It's business as usual, someone says.
Is anybody left to mind the store?
Everything has changed, though nothing has.

The same old buildings huddle in the haze,
with faces at the windows, floor by floor,
the windows they have bolted just in case.

No cause for panic, they maintain, because
the streets go places they have been before.
Everything has changed, though nothing has.

We're still a country that is ruled by laws.
The system's working, and it's quite a bore
that windows have been bolted just in case.

Believe in victory and all that jazz.
Believe we're better off, that less is more.
Everything has changed, though nothing has.
The windows have been bolted just in case.

JAY PARINI

CLOSING COMMENTS

ZACHARY MARCUS: *As we leave this place today, and carry with us*
these sacred words of hope and freedom, of danger and possibility, it
will serve us well to remember the words spoken by President Kennedy
at American University on June 10th of 1963: "So let us not be blind to
our differences, but let us also direct attention to our common interests,
and the means by which those differences can be resolved. And if we
cannot end now our differences, at least we can help make the world
safe for diversity. For in the final analysis our most basic common link
is that we all inhabit this small planet, we all breathe the same air, we
all cherish our children's futures and we are all mortal." Thank you, and
good night.

BIOGRAPHIES

JULIA ALVAREZ emigrated to the United States from the Do-
minican Republic with her parents at the age of ten. She is the author of *How the Garcia Girls Lost their Accents, In the Time of the Butterflies, ¡Yo!, In the Name of Salomé*, and four books of poetry including
Homecoming and *The Other Side/The Other Side*. She has also written
three books for young readers including *A Cafecito Story*, a "green"
fable based on a sustainable farm-literacy project she and her husband, Bill Eichner, have set up in her native country. She is currently
a writer-in-residence at Middlebury College in Vermont.

DAVID BUDBILL's latest CD, *Songs for a Suffering World: A
Prayer for Peace, A Protest Against War*, with bassist William Parker
and drummer Hamid Drake, came out in April 2003. David's most
recent books are *Moment to Moment: Poems of a Mountain Recluse*,
and a revised and expanded edition of his collected poems,
Judevine. Other recent projects include a double CD with William
Parker, *Zen Mountains-Zen Streets: A Duet for Poet & Improvised Bass*,
and a libretto, *A Fleeting Animal: An Opera from Judevine*, for an
opera by Erik Nielsen.

GREG DELANTY was born in Cork, Ireland in 1958. In 1992 he
became an American citizen. He currently teaches at St. Michael's
College in Vermont. His most recent books are *The Hellbox* and *The
Blind Stitch*. Delanty's next book is *The Ship of Birth*. In addition to
writing, he has also translated Aristophanes' *The Knights* (which he
retitled *The Suits*) and Euripedes' *Orestes* for the Penn Complete
Drama Series. Delanty has received numerous awards for his poetry.

JODY GLADDING lives in East Calais, Vermont, and teaches in the Vermont College MFA Program. She also translates French. Her first collection of poetry, *Stone Crop*, appeared in the Yale Younger Poets Series. A chapbook, *Artichoke*, was published by Vermont's Chapiteau Press in 2000. She was the recipient of a Whiting Writers Award.

DONALD HALL received both the National Book Critics Circle Award and the *Los Angeles Times* Book Prize in Poetry for his book, *The One Day*. He also received the Lenore Marshall Award for *The Happy Man*, the 1990 Frost Medal for *Old & New Poems*, and the Ruth Lilly Poetry Prize. He is a member of the American Academy of Arts & Letters, and resides in New Hampshire.

JAMAICA KINCAID was born in St. John's, Antigua. Her books include *At the Bottom of the River, Annie John, Lucy, Autobiography of My Mother*, and *Talk Stories*. In 2000, her book *My Brother* was awarded the Prix Femina Étranger. Kincaid is also the editor of *My Favorite Plant*, a collection of writings on gardens.

GALWAY KINNELL is the author of ten books of poetry including *A New Selected Poems* and translations of Bonnefoy, Villon, and Rilke. He is a former Poet Laureate of Vermont, and has received numerous awards including the National Book Award and the Pulitzer Prize. He lives in Sheffield, Vermont and in New York City, where he teaches in the Graduate Writing Program at New York University.

WILLIAM O'DALY has published six book-length translations of the poetry of Pablo Neruda, as well as a chapbook of his own poetry. Additionally, his poems, translations, essays, articles, and reviews have been published in numerous journals and anthologies. A co-founder of Copper Canyon Press, O'Daly has also taught at Eastern Washington University, Antioch University Seattle, and

Sierra College. Currently, he is collaborating with the writer Hanping Chin on a novel based on the Chinese Cultural Revolution. He resides in California's Sierra foothills with his wife and daughter.

GRACE PALEY was recently named the Vermont State Poet. She is a writer, teacher, feminist, and activist. Her most recent book, *Just As I Thought*, is a collection of both her personal and political essays and articles, and her *Collected Stories* was a finalist for the 1994 National Book Award. Paley lives in Vermont and New York City.

JAY PARINI is a poet, novelist, biographer, and teacher. His books of poetry include *Town Life* and the recently published *House of Days*, and his latest novel is *The Apprentice Lover*. He has also written biographies of Joseph Steinbeck and Robert Frost. Parini teaches literature at Middlebury College in Vermont and lives with his wife and their three sons in Weybridge, Vermont.

RUTH STONE is the author of eight books of poetry, as well as several chapbooks. Her most recent book, *In the Next Galaxy*, won the 2002 National Book Award, and she has received many other honors, including a National Book Critics Circle Award, a Whiting Award, two Guggenheim Fellowships, the Delmore Schwartz Award, Vermont's Cerf Lifetime Achievement Award, *POETRY* Magazine's Bess Hokin Prize, and the Shelly Memorial Award. Stone taught creative writing at many different universities while rearing three daughters alone. She currently resides in Vermont.

ACKNOWLEDGEMENTS

The Publisher wishes to thank all those individuals and companies who so graciously granted permission to reprint the poems in this book.

Anonymous

"How Few of Us Are Left, How Few" from *The Book of Songs*, translated by Arthur Waley. Copyright © 1937/1960 by Grove/Atlantic, Inc. Reprinted by permission of Grove/Atlantic, Inc.

Julia Alvarez

"Poetry Makes Nothing Happen" and "The White House has Disinvited the Poets," copyright © 2003 by Julia Alvarez. Reprinted by permission of Susan Bergholz Literary Services, New York. All rights reserved.

David Budbill

"What Issa Heard" from *Moment to Moment: Poems of a Mountain Recluse* by David Budbill. Copyright © 1999 by David Budbill. Reprinted by permission of Copper Canyon Press, P.O. Box 271, Port Townsend, WA 98368-0271.

Greg Delanty

"A Wake on Lake Champlain" from *Southward*. Copyright © 1992 Louisiana University Press. Reprinted by permission of Oxford Poets Series, Carcanet Press Limited. "The Alien" and "The Skunk Moths" from *The Ship of Birth*. Copyright © 2004 by Greg Delanty. Reprinted by permission of Carcanet Press Limited. "International Call" from *The Blind Stitch*. Copyright © 2002 Oxford Series, Carcanet Press and Louisiana State University Press. Reprinted by permission of Carcanet Press Limited and Louisiana State University Press.

Langston Hughes

"I, Too," "Mother in Wartime," "Official Notice," "Peace," "Harlem (A Dream Deferred)," and "Good Morning" from *The Collected Poems of Langston Hughes* by Langston Hughes, copyright © 1994 by The Estate of Langston Hughes. Used by permission of Alfred A. Knopf, a division of Random House, Inc.

OTHER POETRY TITLES
AVAILABLE FROM
GEORGE BRAZILLER

After Homer
Peter Filkins

Another Language of Flowers
Dorothea Tanning

At Night Beneath the Trees
Michael Krüger

Austerities
Charles Simic

Charles Simic:
   Selected Early Poems
Charles Simic

Charon's Cosmology
Charles Simic

Dismantling the Silence
Charles Simic

The Donner Party
George Keithley

Game in Reverse
Taslima Nasarina

The Illustrations
Norman Dubie

Langston Hughes Reader
Langston Hughes

Lost Body
Aimé Césaire & Pablo Picasso

Making the Skeleton Dance
by Patricia Garfinkel

Poetry of the
   American Renaissance
Paul Kane

Radio Free Queens
Susan Montez

Recovered Body
Scott Cairns

Selected Poems of Rosten
Norman Rosten

Tagore: Final Poems
Rabindranath Tagore

This is the first book set in Hermann Zapf's Optima nova and Optima Titling fonts, produced by Linotype GmbH.
Book designed by Jerry Kelly, New York.